609 LETTER TEMPLATES

Dealing with the Bureaus to Fix Your Credit Score by

Having Everything You Need to Know Explained in Detail

[LUCAS ANDERSON]

Text Copyright © [HENRY RAMSEY]

Legal & Disclaimer

The information contained in this book and its contents is not designed to replace or take the place of any form of medical or professional advice; and is not meant to replace the need for independent medical, financial, legal or other professional advice or services, as may be required. The content and information in this book has been provided for educational and entertainment purposes only.

The content and information contained in this book has been compiled from sources deemed reliable, and it is accurate to the best of the Author's knowledge, information and belief. However, the Author cannot guarantee its accuracy and validity and cannot be held liable for any errors and/or omissions. Further, changes are periodically made to this book as and when needed. Where appropriate and/or necessary, you must consult a professional (including but not limited to your doctor, attorney, financial advisor or such other professional advisor) before using any of the suggested remedies, techniques, or information in this book.

Upon using the contents and information contained in this book, you agree to hold harmless the Author from and against any damages, costs, and expenses, including any legal fees potentially resulting from the application of any of the information provided by this book. This disclaimer applies to any loss, damages or injury caused by the use and application, whether directly or indirectly, of any advice or information presented, whether for breach of contract, tort, negligence, personal injury, criminal intent, or under any other cause of action.

You agree to accept all risks of using the information presented inside this book.

You agree that by continuing to read this book, where appropriate and/or necessary, you shall consult a professional (including but not limited to your doctor, attorney, or financial advisor or such other advisor as needed) before using any of the suggested remedies, techniques, or information in this book.

Table of Contents

CHAPTER 1: Introduction

Basically, a 609 is known as a dispute letter, which you would send to your creditor if you saw you were overcharged or unfairly charged. Most people use a 609 message in order to get the information they feel they should have received. There are several reasons why some information might be kept from you. A 609 letter is sent after two main steps. First, you see that the dispute is on your credit report. Second, you have already filed and processed a debt validation letter. The basis of the message is that you will use it in order to take unfair charges off of your credit report, which will then increase your credit score.

When it is time to report your credit history at all, one of the credit bureaus is going to be responsible for including not only correct information but also the accuracy of the report. The use of this letter in credit repair is going to be based mostly on the idea of whether the credit bureau was responsible for how they verified the information they put onto the report, and if they can do it promptly. Credit bureaus are going to collect information on consumer credit from a lot of different sources like banks. Then they are going to be able to resell that information to any business who would like to evaluate the credit applications of the clients.

Credit bureaus are going to be governed by the FCRA or the Fair Credit Reporting Act, which is going to help detail what credit reporting agencies and information furnishers can and can't do when they decide to report information on the consumer. Using these 609 letters is the right way for us to clean up our credit a bit, and in some cases, it is going to make a perfect situation. However, we must remember that outside of some of the obvious benefits that we are going to discuss, and there are a few things that we need to be aware of ahead of time. Few limitations are going to come with this as well. For example, even after you work with the 609 letters, it is possible that the information will later be seen as accurate could be added to the report again, even after the removal. This is going to happen if the creditor, after the fact, can verify the accuracy. They may take it off for a bit if the 30 days have passed, and they are not able to confirm at that point. But if the information is accurate, remember that it could end up back on the report.

While some people think that it is possible, keep in mind that you are not able to eliminate any obligations to repay a legitimate debt. Even if you write out a 609 letter and you can get that debt removed from the credit report, whether that is for the short term or a longer-term, you still have to pay that legitimate debt. Do not use this to hide from your debts or get from paying them at all. Use this as a method that will help you to clear out some of the older options, or some of the debts that you have taken care of but remain on your reports. Besides, contrary to some of the myths that are out there when it comes to these 609 letters, the FCRA is not going to require that any of the credit agencies keep or provide signed contracts or proof of debts.

You can, however, ask them to give you a description of the procedure that they used to complete the investigation into your accounts. The FCRA, though, is going to give you as a consumer the right to go through and dispute some of the errors that show up on your credit report. This is not a way for you to go through and make some of your student loans or other debts go away, so you do not have to pay them any longer. But it is going to be one of the best ways that you can get information that is not accurately taken off the credit report. We can get a lot of things done when we work with the Section 609 letters, but they are not a magic pill that will make things disappear for us. They will make it easier for us to go through and get rid of information that is not correct and can ensure that we can get rid of debts that maybe we settled in the past but are still harming our credit. This is going to make it easier overall for us to ensure that we can get things organized and get a higher credit score that we are looking for.

How to File a Dispute with 609

It is important to note that there are several template letters for 609. What this means is that you can easily download and use one of these templates yourself. While you usually have to pay for them, there are some which are free. Of course, you will want to remember to include your information in the letter before you send it. You will want to make sure everything is done correctly as this will make it more likely that the information will come off and no one will place it back on your report again.

Make the Necessary Changes to the Letter

This will include changing the name and address. You will also want to make sure your phone number is included. Sometimes people include their email address, but this is not necessary. In fact, it is always safer to only include your home address or PO Box information. You will also want to make sure to edit the whole letter. If something does not match up to what you want to say in your letter, such as what you are trying to dispute on your credit report, you need to state this. These letters are quite generic, which means you need to add in your own information.

CHAPTER 2: What is Section 609 & How Does it Works

Section 609 refers to a section of the Equal Credit Reporting Act (FCRA) that addresses the right to request copies of your own credit reports and related information that appears in your credit reports. Strangely enough, Section 609 has nothing to do with the right to challenge facts about the credit reports or the duty of the credit-reporting agency to examine your disputes. There is no such "609 Conflict Letter" anywhere in the FCRA.

In fact, the FCRA contains a large amount of language that commemorates your rights to challenge the details found in your credit reports. It is, however, in Section 611 of the Legislation, rather than in Section 609. Thanks to section 611, we all have the right to challenge facts that we consider to be inaccurate or unverifiable. And if the information at issue cannot be checked or confirmed, it must be deleted.

Is the 609 Dispute Letter effective?

If you're searching for models for the conflicting text, there's probably a reason for that. Normally, customers send dispute letters to the major credit reporting agencies (Experian, TransUnion, and Equifax) because they feel that something about their credit report is wrong. This can happen if they have applied for a loan or other form of credit, and the lender has told them that they had been denied details on their credit report. It can also happen when they search for their credit report and discover accounts that they don't remember. The practical effect of the dispute letter is that it allows the credit-reporting agency to investigate and correct any reported mistake.

Although there is a lot of information available about 609 Dispute Letters, there is no proof that any particular letter template is more effective than any other letter template. And frankly, you should file your credit report dispute on the back of a beverage napkin and, whether it is legitimate, the details must be changed or deleted. The mode of distribution is essentially meaningless when it comes to your right to an accurate credit report.

Conversely, if the information on your credit reports is correct and verifiable, it is likely to stay on your credit reports. The style of your letter does not change that reality.

Credit scores can range anywhere from as low as 300 all the way up to 850 points. Where you fall on that spectrum can vary from one month to the next based on the information found in your report. Just like with your health, it is your responsibility to make sure that you take care of your credit and if you discover something is wrong, you must take steps to remedy it. To that end, you must know how to manage it properly. To be able to do that, you need to know just how the credit machine works.

You can Google credit repair services, and you'll probably find hundreds of them standing by, ready to take your money to help you get back on the right path. Unfortunately, many of these are scams and the few that are legit, are only telling you the most basic things to do. In many cases, these are things you can do yourself without outside help. Their main goal is to teach you how to fix the things that are wrong.

What they don't do is help you to understand how credit really works and how to prevent yourself from falling into the bad credit trap again.

Understanding Your FICO Score

Almost every creditor will want to see your FICO score before he decides to give you credit. But knowing what the numbers really mean can make a huge difference in managing and taking back control of your financial future. As you gain more knowledge about how the system works, it can empower you. While other factors will weigh in the decision, anyone whose goal is to improve their creditworthiness needs to start with the FICO score as nearly all credit decisions will be based on it.

One of the first things you should understand is the scoring range so you can see what your number really means.

800+ is an exceptional score and is considered to be well above the average. Anyone in this range will find it very easy to get credit approval for just about anything they want. Sadly though, only about 1% of the population falls into this category.

740 – 799 is considered to be very good. While it is not the highest, it is still rated as above average. Anyone in this category will likely qualify for better interest rates and a wide range of credit privileges.

670 – 739 is considered to be good and is about average. They are not the optimum consumer, but they are considered to be in the "acceptable" range.

580 – 669 is considered a fair score. These consumers are usually below average and are labeled as subprime borrowers. This means that while they can get credit, it will be much more difficult for them; interest rates will be higher and they will often have to make higher payments for any purchases they make.

579 – 669 is considered to be a poor score. Consumers who fall in this range are often rejected outright in many places of business. However, they can get credit in altered forms. For example, they may be able to obtain a secured credit card, or they may be required to place a deposit to obtain the approval they need.

This is just a basic guideline of how the FICO score is broken down. Taking into consideration your payment history, the amount of debt you owe, and the type of credit you have will help to determine what your score really is.

It is important to remember, that your credit score does not remain the same throughout your life. Every month, your creditors are submitting new data about your payment activities to the credit bureaus so your score will constantly need adjusting. Also, there are other factors that the Fair Isaac Corporation also factors into your score that may not be as obvious. For example, your income or how long you've been on your job will have little bearing on your credit profile. Also, those who have new credit or a limited history will usually score much lower on the scale than someone who has a longer history of credit to report. This means a low credit score does not necessarily result from missed payments or even being in debt over your heads. Sometimes, it is the result of something entirely out of your control.

In the account history section, which will probably be the most detailed of the entire report, you will find the bulk of the information on you. It will look something like this:

- Creditor name: This could be the name of the merchant or creditor issuing the information.

- Account number: This would be the identifying number of your account. In many cases, this information will be encrypted to protect your privacy and to prevent someone from gaining access to your account information.

- Type of Account: This section will identify if it is a student loan, an auto loan, mortgage, or revolving account (like a credit card).

- Responsibility: Indicates whether you are the only person on the account or if other users are authorized to use it.

- Payment Record: Stipulates what the minimum required payment is on the account.

- Date opened: The exact date the account was established.

- Date reported: The last date the creditor submitted information to the credit bureau.

- Balance: the total amount owed on the account.

- Credit limit: What is the maximum amount of credit you can use.

- High balance or high credit: The highest amount of credit you have used on the account.

- Past due: Total amount of payments past due.

- Payment status: Is the account current, past due, or is it a charge-off (meaning that you haven't paid in a long time and the company does not expect that you will ever pay them).

- Payment history: Indicates how well you've been making payments since the account was opened.

- Collection accounts: This would include any accounts listed that have been sent to a collection agency.

Credit Inquiries

The report will also keep a record of how many times there has been an inquiry into your credit. A lot of inquiries with no new credit issued will reflect very negatively on your score. It is an indication that you have been trying to get credit but have received many rejections, this can make a creditor seriously reconsider taking a chance with you.

There are two different types of credit inquiries you should know about. The first is the "soft" inquiry, which are those made by lenders looking for promotional purposes. Perhaps credit card companies looking for new customers. The second, "hard" inquiries are those creditors that you have actually applied to. Perhaps a bank for credit cards, a department store, or a gas company.

Public Records

The public records section is where you will find information about anything legal in relation to your credit. If you've had a past bankruptcy, any court judgments, tax liens, or anything else it should be included here. However, this is not for everything related to your legal life only things related to your credit. If you've had criminal arrests or convictions, these are not a part of your report unless they have to do with your credit (passing bad checks to pay on your account, for example).

Ideally, you want to make sure that this section of your report is completely clear. Anything in this area will have a major impact on your score and can potentially keep you from getting any type of credit.

The good news is that even if you have a bad report, the negative records do not remain there indefinitely. Most information will remain on your report for 7-10 years. Inquiries will remain for two years max. That means that in time, these negative conditions will eventually drop off and as long as you can maintain a good record, your credit score will naturally improve.

The Fair Isaacs Corporation is very tight-lipped about the exact formula on how they actually calculate the scores, but at least you have a general idea of what they are looking for and what parts of your report need to be boosted to improve your total score.

How to Read Your Report

When you first receive your report, it will probably be a little confusing. Now that you know what each section actually shows though, it will be easier to decipher exactly what it says about you. However, you'll probably want to first give more attention the second section, which will be a detailed description of your payment history.

First, look for any errors or inaccuracies that might have been reported. You would be surprised at just how many of those errors can be found in credit reports – insurance companies saying that the deductible wasn't paid, or that payments were late even when they weren't. Find those errors and mark them. These will be the first items you will address when you're trying to boost your score.

Once you have the errors marked, look for anything that might be fraudulent. Items for credit you don't actually have, for example. These could be a sign that your identity has been compromised and should issues you will want to deal with right away.

When you have all the negative aspects of your credit identified, then it is time to develop a plan of action that will help to improve your score. Because we live in a world that is driven by technology and not actually reasoning people, mistakes occur all the time. False information in your report can bring about deep repercussions and will need to be taken care of immediately. It stands to reason that the sooner you find out these mistakes, the sooner you can do what is necessary to restore your good name and boost your credit score.

Your Credit Utilization Ratio

Finally, you want to look at your credit utilization ratio, which is your credit card balance compared to your actual credit limit. It is important to understand that this ratio will make up a significant part of your FICO score, second only to your payment history.

A high ratio indicates that you might actually be overspending and may be getting in over your head in debt. When creditors see this, they will automatically begin to think that you are a high risk of defaulting on your payments.

When you have a good credit utilization ratio, it can be very instrumental in establishing a good credit score and can actually help to balance out some of those negative aspects of your credit; at least until you start working on removing them.

Ideally, the lower your ratio, the better you look on paper. A ratio of 0% means that you are not using any of your available credit. A credit ratio of 30% or less is what creditors are looking for. Anything above that will cause your overall credit score to drop.

CHAPTER 3: Advice to See Success with 609

Whether you want to delete just one thing from your record or you are looking to delete a lot of different things at the same time, you want to make sure that your 609 Letter is taken care of and ready to go. There are a lot of parts that need to go through in order to get this done, but when you look at some of the templates that we have in the next section, you will see that this is not as bad as it may seem.

When you are ready to write out some of the letters you need to send out to the credit agencies, and you are getting all of the documentation ready to go, make sure to follow some of the general advice that we have below:

Basic Guide to Credit Repair

Damaged credit history and low credit scores can throw a big buckle into your financial life.

You're going to have more trouble getting loans and credit cards than those with good credit. If you get a loan or a credit card, you usually pay a higher interest rate than those with higher credit scores. You will still not be eligible for credit cards with the highest rewards and benefits.

But if you have bad credit, don't despair – there are a variety of realistic ways to start reversing your condition and back on track to good credit. There are six main measures involved in the repair of your credit:

- Assess the credit condition

- Dispute incorrect facts about the credit report

- Pay off your loans

- Learn more about healthy credit habits

- Develop a new loan

- **Wait**

You may be able to skip one or two stages, depending on your situation. Even so, it is prudent to recognize the entire mechanism in the event of unforeseen financial challenges recurring in the future.

Step 1: Assess your credit condition

Check your three credit reports and ratings before taking steps to boost your less-than-stellar credit. You need to understand why your credit scores fell in the first place.

You probably already have a clear idea of what happened, whether you skipped credit card payments or you defaulted on a personal loan. Irrespective of that, taking a thorough, truthful look at your financial condition is the first step on the road to high credit. It also offers a valuable opportunity to find and refute incorrect details that could harm your ratings.

Here's an idea of how you're supposed to go about this phase:

1. Check your credit scores. You should be able to check the credit score for each of your reports free of charge. You might be able to display the score with your credit card. If not, many online services can grant you access to a free credit score by simply signing up.

2. Examine your credit reports. Although your credit scores offer a valuable insight into your condition, credit reports provide a comprehensive image that can make it easier to identify the exact issues at play. List any potentially negative details you find, including late payments, collection accounts, requests, and credit cards with high balances relative to their limits.

3. Build an Action Plan. Once you've checked your documentation to decide what you need to do, browse through the steps listed below and resolve each problem with the required solution.

If you think you're too far to work it out on your own, take credit advice. Credit counselors offer credit-related advice that might prove invaluable in helping you navigate the muddy waters of debt.

Step 2: Incorrect Dispute Details

If you discover any inaccuracies when looking through your credit reports, you have the legal right to appeal to them. When you challenge an account, the credit bureau must investigate and delete the item from your credit report if it is not checked as correct.

In certain cases, a deletion could raise your credit score if the deleted item was negative. But even if the deletion doesn't increase your ranking, it's still important to ensure that all information on your records is correct.

For example, a positive mortgage account that doesn't belong to you does not harm your credit score. But it might make it impossible to borrow in the future because it appears like you owe more money than you do on paper.

Disputing a credit report item is fairly easy. Start by deciding which information is incorrect. Then decide which credit office is reporting errors. Follow these moves, eventually:

- **Submit a 609-default letter by certified mail (return receipt requested) to the authorized credit bureau.** Request clarification of the details you believe is inaccurate. Your disagreement would not guarantee the deletion of the information but allows the office to verify the quality of the information.

- **Wait for a reply.** The procedure can take a month or more. After the review, the office should delete the inaccurate details from your credit report if it cannot be checked.

- **If your conflict has not achieved the settlement you were looking for, you have more options.** You can follow up with the office, contact the creditor who supplied the data, make a report to the Consumer Financial Protection Bureau, or even talk to a consumer protection lawyer if the situation so requires.

If you've already found whole accounts that you don't recognize in your credit reports, consider reporting the incident to the FTC and take careful steps to help avoid problems like identity fraud in the future.

We suggest credit screening, even though you haven't found something out of the ordinary in your credit reports. Credit monitoring systems warn you to changes in your credit reports, helping you detect fraudulent accounts and unauthorized access to credit.

If you are disturbed and concerned about theft, you may also want to freeze your credit reports to prevent credit claims from being made on your behalf until your reports have been thawed. All three major credit bureaus must have freezes free of charge.

Credit locks are a different choice. They are similar to freezes but may have more convenient features, such as instant locking/unlocking capabilities.

Step 3: Pay down debts

Paying down your current debts is, at the same time, one of the hardest and most critical aspects of the credit repair process. It's almost always going to take a lot of time, effort, and (of course) money. But once you have made peace with your debts, you may lay the groundwork for future prosperity.

The amount of debt you owe (especially the use of your credit card) is 30 percent of your FICO score. Paying down your credit card debt is also a very successful way to boost your credit score.

Ready to get started, huh? Here are a few solutions for debt reduction:

Pay outright

If your debts are still up or down (meaning you haven't gone to default yet), you might be able to come up with a strategy to start reducing your balances. This can stop bleeding before you get out of control with your credit situation. Sometimes, you can only need to change your budget and prioritize your debt differently.

Set of collection accounts

It's worth mentioning that you should show caution when paying back old collection accounts. If you do not pay the debt, the creditors, and collection companies who buy the debt will have the right to sue you. However, as the debt grows older, it may become time-barred. When the debt has been time-barred, the debt collector will no longer prosecute you.

In every state, the time-barred debt clock is different.

If you make a small payment on a time-barred debt, you will be able to restart the collection clock. In other words, a single payment could open the door to a future lawsuit against your remaining unpaid balance. So, if you're looking to settle an old collection account, it's usually better to wait until you've saved a full, lump-sum settlement balance first. You may need to talk to a consumer debt counsel for advice.

Eventually, even though you pay or settle a collections account, don't expect your credit scores to leap automatically. Unless the lender uses a newer score model (such as FICO 9), paid collections will continue to harm your credit scores as long as the account is on your record.

The good news, though, is that as collections get older, your credit is becoming less and less impacted. Within seven years from the date of default on the original account, all collections must be removed from your credit report.

Step 4: Learn responsible credit habits

When you've got a deal on unpaid loans, late payments, and heavy credit card balances, take the time to inform yourself of the various ways you can make sure you never get to grips with those issues again.

Making all payments in time

This is a little obvious, but you can never miss a loan or a credit card payment unless you can't stop it. Payment history is one of the most influential variables in many models of credit ratings.

Minimum payments are appropriate if you are just trying to prevent late fees, but we highly suggest that you pay your entire credit card balances every month to prevent interest charges (unless you have a 0 percent rate). This applies mainly to transactions, however, as cash advances and balance transfers typically begin to accrue interest immediately.

We also suggest that you trigger automatic payments so that you never have to leave your way to make a payment before its due date. Only keep an eye on your online account to ensure that payments are still made.

Late payments cannot be reported to credit bureaus until they are at least 30 days late, so you can face late fees and/or other repercussions with the lender from the moment you're late.

After the 30-day waiting period has expired, late payment is likely to be reported to consumer credit bureaus. A new late payment on your credit report would almost definitely hurt your credit scores.

Keep your credit card balances down

The ratio of your total credit card debt to your credit limits is called credit utilization. Credit usage plays a crucial role in your credit score.

For example, the modern FICO Score 8 calculates 30% of your credit scores from the sums you owed in the credit report category. Your use of credit is the most significant aspect considered here.

Vantage Score 3.0 is taking a different approach. It uses credit usage for 20 percent of its ranking formula and the overall debt for 11 percent.

That doesn't mean that the rack up of huge credit card charges during the month would automatically harm you, though. As long as your balances are paid out before the closing date of the statement, your credit utilization ratio should stay low without any harm to your ratings.

Don't borrow more than you can afford

Never borrow so many funds that you can't pay for it in a timely manner. We highly suggest paying off credit card balances in full every month. If you can't stick to paying your credit cards in full every month, you should also stop wiping them out when you're trying to restore your credit.

It's the same with loans. If you're not completely sure you're going to be able to afford a monthly payment without concern, the loan is probably not the right option.

Step 5: Build a new credit

If you've paid off and/or negotiated old debts, you've dealt with incorrect credit details in your reports, and you've built a sound approach to how to deal with credit in the future. You may be able to start creating new credit accounts.

There are a variety of ways to develop new loans. We're going to lead you through some of the best choices, usually available to individuals with low credit scores.

Be an approved consumer

Find a trustworthy friend or family member with a clear history of absolute, on-time payments and ask to be added to his or her credit card account as an approved user.

You can get an approved user card to actually use it, or you can connect it, but you can't give it a card at all. Payment information for your account (positive or negative) will usually also appear on your credit reports either way. Some card issuers do not disclose approved user accounts to the credit bureau.

There may be conditions that prohibit you from being an approved consumer. However, there is usually no need for a credit check.

Open your credit card

There are some credit cards that you are likely to apply for, even though your credit scores are very poor. Most of them have been secured.

Sure, you can need to make a refundable deposit and pay for a card that lacks rewards and benefits. However, credit cards are also among the most valuable tools to restore credit.

Try a loan from a credit builder

Credit builder loans are designed to help you build or repair your loan. You make equal monthly payments all the way through the life of the loan, but you don't get the cash upfront. Instead, you will collect the funds after the balance is paid out in full. Usually, you're going to have to pay interest and some penalties, but none of them appears to be too high.

Credit builders' loans can be very useful on their own. They also fit well alongside other strategies, such as secured credit cards. Using both forms of credit together adds to your wide range of accounts, and a good combination of credit will help your ratings.

Step 6: Wait

Generally speaking, the only thing that can eradicate accurate derogatory details from your credit reports is time. Late fees, collection accounts, and other derogatory items will normally stay on your credit records for 7–10 years. In rare situations, you might be able to eliminate legitimate late fees, but you should not be relying on them. There's always nothing to do with negative credit entries except wait until they're deleted from your records.

Luckily, the negative effect of credit information on your credit score continues to decrease as the information gets older. You're definitely going to see your credit scores go up until the information is deleted from your reports (all other factors being equal), but there's a fair chance they're going to rise progressively even before that.

It will also take time to feel the benefits of your new accounts and good actions. The trick is to be careful and stick to your plans. While remaining responsible, even those with the worst credits will ultimately apply for attractive loans and better credit cards at high rates.

Understanding Credit Repair

We all know that your credit score is one of the greatest determinants of the kind of lifestyle you are likely to lead; that's why we do everything in our power to ensure that we keep it favorable because that in itself determines how much it would cost us to borrow.

It is your right to have correct information reported on your credit report. Why would anybody want to have bad credit owing to wrong and erroneous entries? Is it fair for the individual to have a bad score without any mistakes of his own? Of course not! And for this, you need to take the right steps to fix your bad credit rating. Actually, the Fair Credit Reporting Act (1971) clearly puts it that you have the right to dispute entries in your credit report. You also have a right to get a free copy of your credit report every year, which means that you can check what information has been included in your credit report within that period.

Although the law doesn't clearly tell you to dispute incorrect, erroneous and unverifiable entries, the fact that you have the free copy of your credit report means that you can identify anything that you are uncomfortable with and file a dispute. This is only meant to help you with your credit score and make you more reliable to creditors. You cannot sit back and wait for your credit to fix itself and as soon as you spot errors, you must get to having them fixed.

This coupled with the fact that the FTC clearly states that you can **improve your credit score by yourself** means that all hope is not lost as far as fixing your credit is concerned. Even if the law doesn't tell you to file a dispute if you find any erroneous, inaccurate and unverifiable

34

entries in your credit report, it provides an enabling environment for you to dispute. So you can start to approach the authorities to help you have the errors removed or your score fixed through some means.

For instance, the fact that numerous laws have been put in place to enable credit providers to deal with identify theft and fraud alerts means that you really have some legal backing to ensure that accurate information is published on your credit report. It is your right to have the right score and no one can stop you from having the correct figures mentioned.

The Fair Credit Reporting Act clearly states that it is the duty of every creditor to validate the accuracy or validity of any data contained in a credit report once a credit consumer disputes that information. This means that once you file a dispute on erroneous, inaccurate or unverifiable entries, the creditor will have to validate it or have it removed from the report. This will automatically help you fix your credit score.

Many people wonder if this validation will show badly but it will not. If some erroneous entries were made without your knowledge then you have all the right to challenge it and have it fixed. It will not show badly on your part as you only did something that was necessary for you to rectify a mistake.

I know that sounds fairly straight forward! However, keep in mind that neither the credit reporting agencies nor the credit providers have any interest in having your credit score looking exceptionally good. So they will not jump to help you or themselves take the initiative to fix your problem.

The truth is they make more money when your credit score is bad so why would they want you to have a great credit score when they stand to lose revenues in the process? Everybody thinks for themselves in this world and your creditor will do the same. As long as your account will show bad credit, he or she will be glad to serve you and pull as much money from you as possible. But if they have a chance to help you fix your bad score then they will be least bothered as it will affect their business.

All credit reporting agencies are privately owned multibillion-dollar corporations whose number one priority is profits; they care less about you having a good FICO score. This means that they will definitely want to sabotage your efforts geared towards disputing entries in the credit report; that's why I compiled this book to help you get through the entire dispute process easily and allow you a chance to take the right steps in fixing your bad credit. But do not panic. Although they will put in efforts to block yours, they might not always succeed. You are in the right and they are in the wrong, so it will be easier for you to win the battle. You need to take the right steps and you will get a chance to fix your bad credit score.

To start with, you have to understand how the credit system works, how you can beat the OCR and e-OSCAR computer systems that the credit reporting agencies use, how to use the Fair Credit Reporting Act to your benefit and how to use other effective credit repair strategies to fix your credit. Many times, just fixing your mistakes will do the trick and your credit score will improve instantly. Add to it getting rid of any erroneous entries and you will have a chance to have an extremely high credit score.

In any case, you are the only one who has interests in keeping your credit score high so you have to know how to do everything on your own!

So, you now understand why you have to keep your credit score high and some basics on whether it is possible to repair your credit. You must remain determined to have your credit fixed no matter what the circumstances. However, it is one thing to know that the law is on your side as far as disputing inaccurate, unverifiable and erroneous entries is concerned and another to actually get those entries removed from your credit report. Just by noticing that there is a mistake will not help it in getting solved.

You need to take steps to correct it. It will be quite a process and you will have to gear all your efforts towards cleaning your credit score. It can sound like a daunting task but you need to do it in order to avail a good score. To enable you a clear understanding, let me explain how this is so by showing you how the credit system works.

Credit Score Myths Explained

There are a ton of credit score myths out there, and I don't want you to be fooled. Because in the game of raising your credit score, falling prey to the wrong myth could cost you valuable points on your credit score!

1. A Higher Income Will Raise My Credit Score

In actuality, your income has absolutely zero effect on your credit score. Not everyone has the earning power of Donald Trump, and it's only fair that we are not judged based on how much we earn. What's important to lenders is not what you earn, but how you handle your financial obligations.

2. 'X' Number of Credit Accounts Is Too Many

According to FICO, there is no magic number of credit accounts that is too many. Every person's credit history is different, and consequently, the number of credit accounts that is too many is not set in stone. So don't let anyone tell you different!

Tom is able to maintain his high credit score with seven credit cards, two lines of credit, and five mortgages. But he uses only a small percentage of available credit on his credit cards plus pays them off in full each month. He does not use his lines of credit since they are only for emergencies. And the mortgages are for his investment properties and the payments are always submitted on time.

James has a bunch of credit cards, plus more than one line of credit and mortgages too — but his credit score is low. He has five credit cards that are maxed out (plus he often misses payments), and two lines of credit that are also maxed out. His mortgage payment for his home was 60 days late last time. And at least once a year he's late making the mortgage payment for his cabin in the woods.

In this scenario, Tom has more credit accounts but has a higher score.

Anna has six credit cards that are all maxed out, and she's been late making payments on and off for the past year. She also has a car loan but just barely manages to scrape up enough money to make the payments each month.

Melanie has one credit card, only uses a small percentage of her available balance, and always pays it off on time. She also has a small car loan for which payments are made on time, every time.

In this case, it is Melanie, with the lower number of credit accounts, who has a higher score.

So if you remember nothing else, remember this: The number of accounts you have is less important than what you do with them.

3. Rent is Reported on My Credit Report

The only time your rent could affect your credit report is if you don't pay it and your landlord gets a judgment against you or sends it to a collection agency. That being said, most lenders do take into account mortgage or rent payments when trying to decide if you qualify for their loan product — it's just that this information does not come from your credit report.

4. Cell Phone Payments Are Reported on My Credit Report

It turns out that most cell phone companies don't bother to report to the credit reporting agencies. The exception to this rule is if you don't make the payments and they're sent to a collection agency — that, on the other hand, is very likely to show up on your credit report.

5. My Full Employment History Is on My Credit Report

While your credit report is likely to show the name of your most recent employers, all of the details surrounding your employment will not be there.

6. Closing Old and Inactive Accounts Will Raise My Score

No way! In fact, closing old and inactive accounts might actually lower your score temporarily.

7. Lowering the Credit Limits on My Credit Cards Will Raise My Score

This is another one that gets a big NO WAY! Just as with closing old and inactive accounts, this might actually lower your score.

8. If I Co-Sign on a Loan, It Won't Show Up on My Credit Report

Even though the loan is technically not yours, because you are the lender's "back-up plan" if the other person named on the loan fails to pay, both the loan and payment history will show up on your credit report as if it **is** your loan. So be careful who you co-sign for since any mistakes they make could lower your credit score.

The only way to stop it from showing up on your credit report is to convince the creditor to remove you as a co-signer — but this is easier said than done, so if you ever co-sign on a loan for someone, assume that you're stuck on there until it's 100% paid off!

9. Paying Off Debt Will Boost My Score by X Amount of Points

Don't get me wrong, paying off debt can definitely improve your credit score. But if you ever read something like "pay off your car loan and your credit score will rise by 50 points," assume this is not accurate. Because credit scores are based on so many factors, it's impossible to predict exactly how much of an impact a single change can make. So don't be fooled by those types of promises!

10. My Score Will Drop If I Check My Own Credit

There are two main kinds of credit inquiries: hard and soft.

Hard inquiries generally do lower your credit score. Hard inquiries include those made by your bank before they approve you for your mortgage, or by a credit card company prior to approving you for one of their cards.

Caution: Keep in mind that checking your own credit score is only a soft inquiry if you order it directly via an approved site such as **www.AnnualCreditReport.com**, or via one of the credit bureaus and their affiliated sites. Whereas if you ask your banker to check the score for you, then it will likely count as a hard inquiry, and will lower it.

11. When I Get Married, the Credit Reports of My Spouse and Myself Will Merge

If you value your independence, you'll be happy to know that getting married does not mean giving up your individual credit score. You keep yours, and your spouse keeps theirs. One does not affect the other. However, keep in mind that if you take on joint debts, such as a mortgage, then that mortgage and its payment history will show up on both of your credit reports.

12. Shopping for a Loan Will Lower My Credit Score

Have you ever tried to do the responsible thing by shopping around for the best rate, and worried that you'd be unfairly penalized for doing so due to all those people checking your credit in a short period of time? Worry no more, my friend!

It turns out that the credit reporting agencies are smart enough to know that this is not a big deal. If all of the inquiries are made in a short amount of time, they will usually appear as only one hard inquiry on your report (sometimes two). VantageScore even goes so far as to say that they count all inquiries made within a 14 day period as a single inquiry. So there you go!

13. If I Always Pay My Bills on Time, I'll Have a Perfect Credit Score

It turns out that just paying your bills on time is not enough to guarantee a perfect score. You also have to maintain a desirable mix of credit accounts, have a history of sufficient length, and have an optimal ratio of debt to available credit, among other things. You're not alone if this bums you out — many people are surprised by this one.

But the good news is that anything over 750 is considered excellent. And whether you have a score of 750, or a perfect 850, you're highly likely to get the same great rates when applying for credit.

CHAPTER 4: How to Proceed with the Letters

Now that we know a little bit more about the Section 609 and how we are able to use this for some of our own needs when it is time to handle our credit report and get the different parts to increase, it is time to look at how we can proceed with these letters.

In the following section, we are going to take a look at the steps that you can utilize in order to write out one of these Section 609 letters. But then it is time to figure out what we want to do with them when the letter is written. There are a few different ways that we are able to make sure these letters get back to the right parties, and we are going to take a look at all of them below:

Emails

Our world seems to run online all the time, and finding ways to work on our credit scores and not have to waste a lot of time copying things or worrying about the paper trails can seem like a great idea. And in some cases, we may find that sending in our 609 letters through email is going to be the best situation for our needs.

Before you do this, though, make sure that you take the time and do the proper research. You want the forms to end up in the right locations, rather than getting sent to the wrong departments, and not doing anything for you in the process. Most of the time there will be listings for the various departments that you want to handle and work with for each credit agency, so take a look at those.

Again, when you are ready, you need to have as many details ready to go for this as possible. Just sending in a few lines about the process and thinking that will get things done is foolish. Write out a letter just like you would if you planned to send these by mail, and use that as the main body of your email. Mention Section 609 and some of the disputes that you want to bring up.

In addition to this, you need to take some time adding in the other details. Attach some ways to prove your identity to the email, along with a copy of the credit report that has been highlighted to show what is going on and what you would like to dispute. Add in any of the other documentation that is needed to help support your case, and have it as clean and organized as possible to make sure the right people can find it and will utilize this information to help you out.

Doing it All Online

Many of the credit agencies have made it easier to go through and work on some of these claims online. This helps you out because you will not need to go through and print it all off or worry about finding the paperwork or printing a bunch of things off. And if you are already on your credit report, your identification has been taken care of.

Since so many people are online these days, doing this right from the credit report is a simple and easy process to work with, and you will catch onto it fairly quickly. Don't take the easy way out with this. If you just click on the part that you think is wrong and submit a claim on it, this is not enough. There won't be any reference back to Section 609, and you will not be able to get them to necessarily follow the rules that come with Section 609.

This is where being detailed is going to be useful in the long run. When you do submit one of these claims online, make sure that you write a note with it to talk about Section 609, specifically the part of 609 that you want to reference in this dispute. You can usually attach other forms to document, who you are and why you think these need to be dropped. Treat this just like you would if you tried to mail the information to the credit agency. The more details that you are able to include in this, the better. This will help to build up your case and can make it harder for those items to stay on your credit report for a long period of time. Make sure to mention the 30-day time limit as well.

Telephone

A telephone is one method that you can use, but it is not usually the right one for this kind of process. For example, how easy is it going to be to show the credit agency what your driver's license looks like? You can repeat the number over if you would like, but this process is still a bit more laborious than some of the others and doesn't always work as well as we would hope it could.

However, this is definitely an option that we can use in order to reach the credit agencies, and for some people who are not sure of what their rights are, or would rather talk directly to the individuals in charge about this issue, the telephone can be the right option. Make sure that you have a copy of your credit report in front of you when you start and having some other identification information and more. This will ensure that you are prepared when someone comes on the line to speak with you.

Just like we will show when working on our letter templates, later on, we need to make sure that we speak about the issue at hand, explain our rights, and go through the information on Section 609. There is the possibility that the other side is going to have some questions for you, and they will at least want to go through and verify your identity to make sure they are ready to go. But the same rules apply here, and if you don't get a response within 30 days of that phone call, then the information should be erased.

Keep good records of what is discussed in that conversation, who you talked to during that time, what time and date it was, and so on. This will make it easier to get someone to respond to you and can help us to get this to work in our favor. Also, remember that you will need to repeat these phone calls to all three credit bureaus in order to get your information cleared on all of them.

Mail

Another option that you are able to work with is mail. This is usually a good method to use because it allows you a way to send in all of the information at once. Since you probably already have a physical copy of your SSN, driver's license, the credit report and more, you can get copies of these made pretty quickly, and then send them on with the Section 609 letter that you are working with. This method also allows us a way to go through and circle or highlight the parts of our credit report that we want to point out to the credit reporting agency.

This method is quick and efficient and will make sure that the information gets to the right party. You can try some of the other options, but sometimes this brings up issues like your information getting lost in the spam folder or getting sent to the wrong part. Mail can take some of that out of the way and will ensure that everything gets to the right location at the right time.

Certified Mail

For the most part, you are going to find that working with certified mail is going to be one of the best options that you can choose. This will ensure that the letter gets to the right place and can tell you for certain when the 30-day countdown is going to begin.

If you send this with regular mail, you have to make some guesses on when the letter will arrive at the end address that you want. And sometimes you will be wrong. If there is a delay in the mailing and it gets there too late, then you may start your 30 days too early. On the other hand, if you assume it is going to take so many days and it takes less, you may wait around too long and miss your chance to take this loophole and use it to your advantage.

Certified mail is able to fix this issue. When the credit agency receives the letter, you will get a receipt about that exact date and even the time. This is going to make it so much easier for you to have exact times, and you can add these to your records. There is no more guessing along the way, and you can be sure that this particular loophole is going to work to your advantage.

Another benefit that comes with certified mail is that you make sure that it gets to its location. If you never get a receipt back or get something back that says the letter was rejected or not left at the right place, then you will know about this ahead of time. On the other hand, if it does get to its location, you will know this and have proof of it for later use. Sometimes things get lost. But you want to be on the winning side of that one. If the credit agency says that they did not receive the letter, you will have proof that you sent it and that someone within the business received it and signed for it. Whether the company lost it along the way, or they are trying to be nefarious and not fix the issue for you, the certified mail will help you to get it all to work for you.

When it comes to worrying about those 30 days and how it will affect you, having it all in writing and receipts to show what you have done and when it is going to be important, this can take out some of the guesswork in the process and will ensure that you are actually going to get things to work for you if the 30 days have come and gone, and no one will be able to come back and say that you didn't follow the right procedures.

As we can see, there are a few different options that we are able to use when it comes to sending out our Section 609 letters.

CHAPTER 5: The 5 Templates You Need

Template 1

We also want to make sure that you can have as many of these templates available that work for you. You could try sending a different one to each of the three credit agencies if that works the best for you, or you can choose to send the same one to all three. No matter what options you are considering here, we need to make sure that we are able to get a lot of choices in the process. Here is the fifth template letter that you can consider using for your needs.

Date

Your Name

Your Address

Your current city, state, and zip code.

Complain Department

Name of Credit Bureau (You can pick which one goes here)

Address

Dear Sir or Madam

I Take this time to identify all of the items that you would like to dispute, going by the name of the source including whether they come from a tax court or creditors and so on. You can even identify the type of item that you refer to, such as a judgment, a credit account, and more.

Please take the time to investigate this matter and delete the disputed items. As per Section 609 mentioned above, you have 30 days from the receipt of this letter to respond, or the item must be removed. I appreciate your speed in this matter.

Sincerely

[Add your signature to this part]

[Print your name here]

*Make sure that you attach copies of your proof of identity, including your birth date, name, SSN, and your current mailing address. You also want to attach a copy of your credit report, making sure that you highlighted all of the relevant items to make it easier for the interested parties to see what you are talking about.

Template 2

This is the primary format that we will invest some energy in. It will incorporate the entirety of the various parts that you need to get the message to the correct gatherings, and it is quite basic. Recollect that this is only a layout, and we can go through and utilize this as a guide or a blueprint. On the off chance that it doesn't by and large coordinate with what you need, you can roll out certain improvements, or you can decide to utilize one of different layouts that we will have accessible.

Name

Address

Telephone Number

Record # (make a point to incorporate this on the off chance that you have that data).

Name of the Company Contacting/Point of Contact Person

Important Department

Address

Date

Dear [Include the name of the credit revealing office or utilize the name of the contact party in the event that you approach this information]

I'm composing today to practice my entitlement to scrutinize the legitimacy of the obligation your office claims I owe, compliant with the FCRA, Fair Credit Reporting Act.

As expressed in Section 609 of the FCRA, (2) €:

"A customer revealing office isn't needed to eliminate precise harsh data from a purchaser's record except if the data is obsolete under Section 609 or can't be checked."

Just like my right, I am mentioning confirmation of the accompanying things:

[This is the place where we will list any of the things that we are hoping to debate, including the entirety of the record names and numbers that have been recorded with your credit report]

Furthermore, I have featured these things on the joined duplicate of the credit report I got.

I demand that all future correspondence be done through the mail or email. As expressed in the FCRA, you are needed to react to my debate inside 30 days of receipt of this letter. In the event that you neglect to offer a reaction, all contested data should be erased.

Much obliged to you for your brief regard for this matter.

Earnestly,

[Add your mark to this part]

[Print your name here]

See appended; [This is the place where you will rattle off the entirety of the archives that you will connect with this letter]

*Make sure that you join duplicates of your verification of personality, including your introduction to the world date, name, SSN, and your present street number. You additionally need to join a duplicate of your credit report, ensuring that you featured the entirety of the significant things to make it simpler for the invested individuals to perceive what you are discussing.

Template 3

There are a ton of times when the primary format that we talked about will be sufficient for your necessities and can assist you with completing the entirety of the work. Then again, it could be conceivable that you need to discuss the debate in an alternate way, or you just didn't care for the arrangement or something different about the other layout that we went through. That is okay. The accompanying layout will be the one that we can work with too. It discusses a ton of the very issues that we did above however will have a couple of different parts added to it to make this work too. The second format that we can work with incorporates:

Name

Address

Telephone Number

Record # (make a point to incorporate this in the event that you have that data).

Name of the Company Contacting/Point of Contact Person

Important Department

Address

Date

Dear Sir or Madam

I'm writing to practice my entitlement to debate the accompanying things on my document. I have caused a note of these things on the joined duplicate of the report I to have gotten from your organization. You will likewise discover connected duplicates of reports that help to show my personality, SSN, birthdate, and current location.

As expressed in the FCRA, or Fair Credit Reporting Act, Section 609:

[This will be the segment where we incorporate a couple of pertinent statements that depend on what space of Section 609 you might want to debate at that point. You can return to the past section to perceive what a portion of these statements are about, or you can go to the FTC's site to get the authority report that has the specific verbiage that you need. Recollect that you need to note which of the sub-segments you are citing from as well].

The things that I wish to question are as per the following:

1.   [This is the part where you will incorporate however many significant things as you can. You can have up to 20, yet attempt to just work with the ones that bode well for you].

2.   [Keep as a main priority that the subtleties will be the most significant with this one. You need to incorporate the name and the quantity of the record, as recorded on your credit report]

These are [inaccurate, wrong, unverified] because of the absence of approval by various gatherings that is needed by Section 609. I have appended duplicates of important documentation.

I would see the value in your help with researching this way inside the following 30 days. As needed by the FCRA, on the off chance that you neglect to do as such, all previously mentioned data/questioned things should be erased from the report.

Genuinely:

[Add your mark to this part]

[Print your name here]

See connected; [This is the place where you will drill down the entirety of the records that you will append with this letter]

*Make sure that you append duplicates of your verification of personality, including your introduction to the world date, name, SSN, and your present postage information. You likewise need to connect a duplicate of your credit report, ensuring that you featured the entirety of the significant things to make it simpler for the invested individuals to perceive what you are discussing.

Template 4

We have investigated some truly genuine instances of the format that you can use with regards to working with Section 609 and ensuring that you can get the credit offices to delete a portion of the awful stuff that is on your reports and causing you a ton of issues en route. In any case, we will investigate a third layout that we can use also.

You will see that this one will be really like what we have done in the last two, yet there are some various approaches to introduce the data and various words that are being utilized also. We should investigate this model and perceive how it very well may be comparable or not the same as the other two layouts that we are working with:

Name

Address

Telephone Number

Record # (make a point to incorporate this in the event that you have that data).

Name of the Company Contacting/Point of Contact Person

Applicable Department

Address

Date

To the responsible party in question,

This letter is a proper debate as per the Fair Credit Reporting Act (FCRA).

Endless supply of my credit report, I have discovered that there are a few off base and unconfirmed things. These have adversely affected my present capacity to get credit, and have given pointless shame and bother.

As I am certain you know, it is my right, as indicated by Section 609 of the FCRA, to demand a legitimate examination concerning these errors. Specifically, I am referring to Section 609 (c) (B) (iii), which records "the privilege of a purchaser to question data in the document of the buyer" under the "model synopsis of the privileges of shoppers."

All things considered, coming up next are things I wish to question on my credit report:

1.   [This is the part where you will incorporate however many applicable things as you have. You can do up to 20. Ensure that you incorporate the name and the number that is recorded on each record on this report.]

I have additionally featured the entirety of the things that are pertinent to the appended duplicate of the said credit report.

As expressed in the FCRA, you are needed to react to my debate inside 30 days of receipt of this letter. In the event that you neglect to offer a reaction, all contested data should be erased. I have connected all the significant documentation for your audit. I thank you ahead of time for your brief reaction and goal of this issue.

Truly

[Add your mark to this part]

[Print your name here]

See joined; [This is the place where you will drill down the entirety

*Make sure that you connect duplicates of your evidence of character, including your introduction to the world date, name, SSN, and your

present street number. You additionally need to connect a duplicate of your credit report, ensuring that you featured the entirety of the applicable things to make it simpler for the invested individuals to perceive what you are discussing.

Template 5

This will be a somewhat unique sort of letter than what we saw previously. This will be significant in light of the fact that it assists us with following up on the off chance that we have not heard a single thing from the other party. Recall that we are allowing them 30 days to go through and give us a reaction or the like, or they naturally need to take that off their reports. The 30 days starts when they get the letter you send, not when you compose it or when you send it. This is another motivation behind why it is critical to go through and get it sent through confirmed mail, so you have a precise date close by.

At the point when the 30 days are finished with, the time has come to do a subsequent letter. This will be the point at which you let the organization realize that the 30 days are finished and that you anticipate that things on your report should be deleted and finished with as quickly as time permits. That is the reason we will work with the accompanying to assist us with composing the subsequent letter that we need.

Name

Address

Telephone Number

Record # (make a point to incorporate this in the event that you have that data).

Name of the Company Contacting/Point of Contact Person

Important Department

Address

Date

Dear Sir or Madam

My name is [Your name], and I contacted you a little while back in regards surprisingly report. This letter is to inform you that you have not reacted to my underlying letter, dated [insert date]. I have repeated the provisions of my question beneath for your benefit.

[This is the place where we will embed data from the letter we expounded initially on the contested things. Incorporate questioned account names and numbers as recorded on your credit report.]

Area 609 of the FCRA states that you should explore my debate inside 30 schedule days from my underlying letter. As you have neglected to do as such, I generously demand that you eliminate the previously mentioned things from my credit report.

Any further remarks or questions can be coordinated to my lawful delegate, [insert name], and I can be reached at [insert telephone number].

Genuinely

[Add your mark to this part]

[Print your name here]

See joined; [This is the place where you will rattle off the entirety of the reports that you will connect with this letter]

*Make sure that you connect duplicates of your evidence of character, including your introduction to the world date, name, SSN, and your present street number. You additionally need to append a duplicate of your credit report, ensuring that you featured the entirety of the pertinent things to make it simpler for the invested individuals to perceive what you are discussing

CHAPTER 6: Conclusion

After this guide, you should have enough confidence to take complete control of your financial status and your credit report. It must have been very difficult for you to delete things from your credit report, or you have given up on the fact that it is impossible to raise your credit score. I've made sure you're going to be so confident with the guide that you can take things out of your credit report. Your credit score goes hand-in-hand with your financial security, and there's nothing more rewarding than living a stable life. You should be able to know and assess what your credit score is and how you can improve it. You should be able to know what to do while fixing your credit score, and even what not to do with it.

You can try out the creditors, and you can do so by sending letters of goodwill, with the promises I made to help you increase your FICO score, and also to fix your credit. You should be able to do that, because I've made a guide to that in the book, and I've also helped you increase your credit score to over 800, which is exceptional. Today's credit background is what will decide whether you're going to get a loan, a career, or even a recommendation. If you've got a poor credit history, it's really going to be terrible if you don't follow the guide I gave it to you. The main purpose of the book is to help you conquer the fear and negativity; if you want to obtain the highest credit score, you need to believe in yourself that you can manage it and raise it to more than 800.

The models are in order to help you make those improvements, a guide for how to write a conflict letter and a 609-credit repair letter. The guide is there to help you stabilize your credit history and your financial future.

CPSIA information can be obtained
at www.ICGtesting.com
Printed in the USA
BVHW091935120521
607126BV00014B/2760